INTRODUCTION

As a church developer, local pastor, and entrepreneur, I struggled to find concise, high-quality materials to help with growth and development for small to mid-size local ministries. I have attended Church Planters Conferences, graduated from the church planter academy, and come from a legacy of church planters. Yet, finding the answer to help my congregation with building ministry post-COVID has been highly challenging and at times overwhelming. The United States has shifted from a somewhat churched culture to a highly unchurched culture. Local ministries are struggling to find relevance and identity with the multi-generational communities they are called to minister to and serve. This results in multi-generational communities having a limited understanding of the benefits of faith and the promises of God.

This workbook is designed to equip local ministries with the tools to build relevance and relationships with multi-generational communities. Without this bridge, local ministries will struggle to create growth and development within their communities. When local ministries value and intersect with multi-generational communities, they experience renewed purpose and a sense of vision—creating greater value, knowledge, wisdom, and capacity to understand how God is working through them to develop disciples of Jesus Christ and revealing God's transformative grace working through their united, organized effort, bringing fulfillment to their lives and relevance to ministry.

However, the local church needs to understand who they are equipped to reach and be willing to become a new ministry transforming with new members to create an advancing ministry.

This workbook is a pathway that creates value, unites, and empowers all generations in developing disciples for Jesus Christ. Creating ministries that are relevant and biblically centered on establishing purpose, family enrichment, and hope to deal with the complexities of life and the uncertainty of our country's future. Yet, there is one fact: that through Christ, all things are possible.

What does a multi-generational ministry look like when they work in tandem to fulfill the great commission of Christ? A ministry where all people possess the "gift of contribution" and are welcomed to use their gift for the continuation of the gospel. The value we place on each other's contributions is based on the needs of the community and our personal assessment of the importance of their gift(s). This process of evaluation provides a ministry where everyone seeks to belong and give actively and wholeheartedly, without judgment or hesitation, as they experience the significance of their generosity to the local ministry.

As followers of Christ, we must show adequate respect for each other's benevolence and properly assign value based on the advancement of the kingdom of God and the local ministry. We are called to love our neighbor as ourselves, and as we do, we discover the true value of one another and embody the true essence of Christ.

As you go through the exercises below, remember that your initial evaluation of others is often based on sight, but relationships determine the real value assessment.

UNDERSTANDING THE VALUE OF INFLUENCE

How do you value the following people below? Five being the highest value and one being the lowest. Circle your answer

Family & Friends 5 4 3 2 1	Christ 5 4 3 2 1	General Contractor 5 4 3 2 1
Neighbor 5 4 3 2 1	Church Member 5 4 3 2 1	Myself 5 4 3 2 1
Spouse/Significant other 5 4 3 2 1	Waitress/Waiter 5 4 3 2 1	Boss 5 4 3 2 1
Co-worker 5 4 3 2 1	Pastor/Pastor Wife 5 4 3 2 1	Others 5 4 3 2 1

Based on your answer above, you will gain a greater understanding of how you view different groups of people and their current importance in your life.

EVALUATION QUESTIONS

On a scale of 1 lowest to 5 highest,

▸ How important are people to you?

▸ If you value people less than a 4 or 5, why would they be interested in coming or joining your church/religious community?

- Based on your current value assessment, can you effectively grow the Kingdom of God and the local church?

- If we view others as three or below, why would they want to be in ministry?

- When recruiting new members, is the church looking to meet the needs of the church or the needs of the people?

- Why do we start with the needs of the church over the needs of the people?

- Define, in your words, the importance of putting the needs of the people before the needs of the church?

- How do we become a church that understands that building relationships is the key to growing the local church?

ANALYZING YOUR TARGET MARKET

Who's your Target

Demographics: Non-Churched-Largest group of people available to evangelize Ex. 67% of people in Leavenworth, KS

Non-churched

They desire to: belong, to be valued, heard, respected, & to contribute

Looking for: communities to which to belong, build quality relationships, to be impactful, inspiring, discover purpose, to create stability, and to build the family unit.

Somewhat Churched

Looking for a spiritual community that meets their needs and provides a space for them to participate, belong, grow, and enrich their families.

Churched

38% of Americans are churched, 11% are loyal to one church, and 27% attend multiple churches

- How relevant is your ministry to meeting the needs of your target audience?

- How will the ministry develop to become more relevant to your target audience?

- Is the target audience capable of being reached by your current resources and relationships?

- Would it be better to concentrate on a target audience that is more relevant to your capabilities or interests?

- How do you plan to maintain ministry morale, energy, vigor, growth, and development throughout the various stages of your transformation?

- What do you believe your transformation stages to be or look like?

- What strategies and benchmarks will be used to identify and measure your transformational progress?

- How will you celebrate your wins with the ministry and community?

UNDERSTANDING THE POWER OF CONTRIBUTION

RELATIONSHIPS

- What relationships do you need to make/have to achieve your goals?
  _____
  _____
  _____

- How will those relationships impact, transform, and enrich others?
  _____
  _____
  _____

- How will these relationships impact, transform, and enrich your family and friends?
  _____
  _____
  _____

- How will these relationships impact, transform, and enrich the kingdom of God and the local ministry?
  _____
  _____
  _____

- How will these relationships impact, transform, and enrich your life?
  _____
  _____
  _____

SPIRITUAL GIFTS

▶ What are your spiritual gifts?

▶ How will your spiritual gifts/talents enrich and build your family and friends?

▶ How will your spiritual gifts/talents enrich and build others?

▶ How will your spiritual gifts/talents enrich and build the kingdom of God and the local ministry?

▶ How will your spiritual gifts/talents enrich and build you?

GENEROSITY

▸ How do you plan to express your generosity?

▸ How will that generosity transform and grow your family and friends?

▸ How will that generosity transform and grow others?

▸ How will that generosity transform and grow the Kingdom of God and the local ministry?

▸ How will that generosity transform and grow you?

JESUS'S PART

▸ In what area are you looking for God to grow and build your family and friends?

▸ In what area are you looking for God to grow and build the local ministry?

▸ In what area are you looking for God to grow and build others?

▸ In what area are you looking for God to grow and build you?

NOTES

CLOSING THOUGHT

Without Faith (Belief that God Can & Will) & Fellowship (Organized effort & Celebration), ministry development would be impossible. As you unite around discovering and executing God's purpose and plan for your ministry, you will experience fulfillment, peace, joy, and excitement. What God is doing through your teamwork will impact and train generations for years to come. Never let this fire go out. God's favor now rests upon you, and through your continued development, you will remain relevant and impactful throughout your ministry experience.

As you encounter difficulties, struggles, and new seasons in ministry, make sure you revisit this process to check for alignment or realignment to God's purpose and plan for your ministry. Remember, through Christ, all things are possible, and only what you do for Christ will last.

Thank you for the opportunity to serve your ministry! I sit in expectation, awaiting to observe how God will use your ministry to create more disciples for Jesus Christ.

Live blessed,

George L. Roath III MDiv.
CEO of TrueMe LLC
georgeroath@Trueme.business
Trueme.business

SCAN FOR ADDITIONAL RESOURCES

BONUS FEATURE 1

Youth & Young Adult Training Course: Creating Relevance

Key Thought: The Promise

1. What guarantees or promises do youth and young adults receive from ministry?

----

2. Are our thoughts on the promise relevant to them?

----

3. If not, how do we guide them to discover how their fruit(s) and the revelation of God's promise to them will transform us?

UNDERSTANDING MINISTRY VALUE

Key Thought: The Promise

1. Why is ministry relevant in my life?

----

2 Why is ministry important to me?

----

3 What will ministry help me to become?

Corporate level

1 Why is my ministry relevant for others?

----

2 Why will this impact be important in their lives?

----

3 How does this impact help others to become what God desires of them in this season?

A Kingdom Approach

1 Why are our ministries relevant to the world?

----

2 Why are our ministries' important to the development of others?

----

3 How will our ministries aid the world in becoming what God intended for us to be?

Development Analyst

1. Do it for me (Baby)
2. I can do it (Adolescent)
3. You can count on me (Adult)

A Training Strategy: The Benefits

1. Delayed Gratification vs Instant gratification
2. Discipline vs No Discipline
3. Purpose & Planning vs Reaction & Circumstances
4. God's Plan vs Desire
5. Fulfillment vs Momentary Happiness

Reflection Questions

Where are they in their development?

_____

_____

How do we help them to graduate to the next level of development?

_____

_____

The Conversation Matters: (With Them and Us)

1. What would make ministry relevant to you?

_____

_____

2. Why is ministry important to the development of your life?

_____

_____

3. Why is your ministry important to the development of my ministry?

_____

_____

4 Why is your ministry important to the development of our ministries?

----

5 How will your ministry transform our local, regional, and international ministries?

----

6 Is this level of impact important to you?

7 If so, what is the best way forward for us to experience the promises of God?

----

8 What educational and discipleship tools are needed, to aid us in becoming relevant to the world and each other?

----

9 What is our accountability plan for becoming what God desires of us?

NOTES

BONUS FEATURE 2

Strategic Planning for an Advancing Ministry

THE MEASURABLES

1. Goals

2. Checkpoints

3. Desired Outcomes

4. Unexpected Outcomes

5. Process of Evaluations, Course Correction (s), and Reflection

6. Follow-up Team

EQUIPPING FOR MINISTRY

① Identify the Target Audience (s) you are equipped to reach

----

② Target Audience(s) desired outcomes

----

③ Timing Study: Discovering when those groups are available and are looking for their desired outcomes

----
----

④ Identify & Build a team with the skills to attract, recruit, and retain your Target Audience(s)

OUTREACH EVENTS: MONTHLY, QUARTERLY, AND ANNUAL

1. Type of Events & Target Audience (s)
2. Partners: local, domestic, government, historical societies, and international
3. Resources: Financial, manpower, time, faith, willpower, and leadership
4. Locations: The place (s) where your target audience visits and lives
5. Facilities: Place (s) where you can gather together
6. Marketing & Advertisement: Online, community, and local ministries

SCAN FOR ADDITIONAL RESOURCES

NOTES

www.ingramcontent.com/pod-product-compliance
Lightning Source LLC
Chambersburg PA
CBHW041431090426
42744CB00002B/28